Troya Bishop, M.Ed.

The Answers to Intimacy:
Why Men NEED Oral Sex
&
Women NEED to Talk

Troya Bishop, M. Ed.

Troya Bishop, M.Ed.

ISBN:
978-0-9821468-5-9

DEDICATION

This book is dedicated to every person who has ever dared to love and to those who dared to love *again* after love or marriage the first time around did not work out as planned.

To those who struggle with intimate connections because the bond of intimacy with your mother is broken: I honor your pain and I share your struggle. Many people do not understand our experiences with love and intimacy. The person who was supposed to teach us about love and connecting deeply could not. Our struggle is real, but we are not alone and we indeed deserve and will have love if we continue to do the work.

It is also dedicated to my daughter Zoe, my god-children, and all of the children of parents who wanted to get love right, but really got it wrong. I pray that is work will help solidify the foundation of marriages of people around the world. May God use it to be a part of a strong foundation that solid families of faith are built on.

Special dedication to those who dared to love ME! My life is better because of those who intentionally loved me. Love and love-lost teaches powerful lessons. I have grown stronger and wiser from every lesson in love I have experienced.

To my future husband: I have been working on myself and learning how to love you. I have studied love, love languages, intimacy and affection. We will live, laugh and love each other and our children forever. I'm so ready!

FOREWORD
By Dr. F. Keith Slaughter

"The text/workbook that Troya has written is a profound and important response to a problem that plagues our people: the problem of communication. Though the provocative title may entice passing interest, the subject matter is grounded in historical, cultural and psychosocial research that is scholarly, practical and needful for the healing of Black couples and families, and which may lead to the resurrection of our people. Troya's Socratic approach to teaching interpersonal communication skills invites the reader to do the work of self-reflection. Through honest confrontation of the sources of pain and brokenness among us we may experience a repair of our most precious relationships. The Answers...actually gives us answers for one of the most pressing problematics plaguing our people."

Dr. F. Keith Slaughter, ThD, is an Associate Professor -Psychology of Religion and Pastoral Care at the world renowned Interdenominational Theological Center in Atlanta, Georgia.

Troya Bishop, M.Ed.

Troya Bishop, M.Ed.

TABLE OF CONTENTS

Troya Bishop, M.Ed.

ACKNOWLEDGMENTS

I acknowledge all of my ancestors who wanted to publicly celebrate their love and could not, because it was illegal. I honor their love for each other, their pain, and the sacrifices they made to preserve their family and their sanity.

I honor Harriet Tubman, who I studied while developing this book project. Like her, I believe that the ultimate way to be free in your mind is through love for your family, spouse and community. Also like Sister Harriet, I believe that sometimes you have to let people go and love them from afar, because freedom ain't free, and everybody ain't willing to pay the cost.

I acknowledge and honor all of the ancestors who pursued academics before me, especially Dr. W.E.B. Dubois and Dr. Naim Akbar. They and many others dared to study the arts and sciences of Black Love.

I honor those whose work I've referenced in this book specifically my SHEro and fellow Bison, Dr. Francis Cress Welsing. Your work and commitment to Black Love and Black Empowerment is amazing and will never be forgotten. Ase'.

PREFACE
THE PURPOSE OF THIS BOOK

The ultimate purpose of this book is to promote love, peace and power through meaningful relationships.   Love is the most powerful entity in this world, so teaching people how to do a better job of loving themselves and each other, is essential in accomplishing the ultimate goal of deep connection and sustained peace.   When I came up with the title of this book, most people who know me were SHOCKED!

I think the initial knee-jerk reaction to the title is surprising to people who know me well, because I typically do not share about my relationships and certainly not about sex or intimate relationships. So whether you know me or not, *relax*. My sex-life is not being shared in this book.   This is not a tell-all personal gossiping book.

This is a book with the word WHY in the title. This is not a book about how, how often, when, where, or anything of the sort as it relates to oral sex or talking to your spouse. To be clear this book will support and deepen your understanding of two **psychological** and **physiological** needs that often cause conflicts in relationships: sex and communication.

My passion for people and a deep-seeded need to speak the truth as I see it are the foundations for this book. *The Answers to Intimacy* is rooted in real peer-reviewed research and feedback I received from the first two books: *The Answers: A Parent's Guide to Discussing Racism with Children* and *The Answers: Discussing and Defeating Racism in America.*

I had no idea when I wrote the first books that conducting workshops, speaking on radio shows, and hosting discussion sessions on social media would lead me to connecting the dots between racism, oppression, sexual expression and the capacity to love. But that is exactly what happened.

Like the other books I've published, this one has an action-guide to assist you and your spouse with self-discovery and discovery with how to deepen the intimacy in your relationship. The action-guide is a section immediately following each chapter. I wanted to be sure that couples do not have an excuse for not walking through the interactive steps. So I eliminated the cost of the additional book, unlike the other two in *The Answers* series. Reading about intimacy is one thing, but taking the time to **apply** what you have read to your life is what this journey of knowledge is all about.

These books will encourage you to grow if you allow them to. Are you changing? Anything that is not changing is not growing. Anything that is not growing is dead! I pray that you and your relationships will grow and thrive. Completing the research and writing for this book certainly forced me to grow and to examine my relationships. The first few chapters were painful to write and to work through. I wholeheartedly believe in the saying, "The truth will set you free, but first it will piss you off"! True indeed.

Often, I cried during the research process and this project kept me up at night. I truly had to consider the areas where *my* relationships needed to grow in order for them to survive. I had forgotten about some pain, and never acknowledged other pain in my family, in my life and in my lineage. Being authentic in this process forced me to work through it all. I pray that you will be brave enough to lean into the pain and work through the pain to enhance your ability to connect on a deeper level with the people in your life.

Finally, thank you for taking this journey of further self-knowledge and self-discovery with me. May you be brave enough to be honest with yourself and your partner. May all of your relationships be made more solid, and may everything you do with a pure heart be blessed! My contact info is included in the, "About the Author Section". Feel free to share your story with me and keep me posted on your progress. God Bless Ya!

CHAPTER ONE
THE HISTORY OF BROKEN INTIMACY BETWEEN AFRICAN AMERICAN MEN & AFRICAN AMERICAN WOMEN

The history of African men, African women and their children being separated by people who had no conscious and no conviction, dates back to the shores of Africa during the 15th century. This is true for Black people in the Caribbean islands, South America and along the coasts of North America where purchasing, enslaving and trading Africans took place. Specifically, enslaved Africans who were brought to America were intentionally separated by governmental agencies historically, until approximately 1970.

According to the African American Intellectual History Society Inc., forced family separation was always a reality in the lives of enslaved African people (Holden, 2018). Enslaved African children were a very lucrative business. The expansion, maintenance, and future of enslaving Africans in America as an economic system depended on these children being separated from their parents. Slave owners used isolation and fear as tactics to control the enslaved African people. This trauma of the separation tactics caused a further breakdown in intimacy and lack of trust between African men, African women and African children. These separation tactics kept the Black family apart, as well as the economic need to have more male than female workers.

The preference for male laborers in the trade of enslaved African people limited the ability of most enslaved African men and women from developing real relationships (Hallam, 2018). In the late seventeenth and early eighteenth centuries when the harsh policies of enslaving Africans were made concretely into law, enslaved African people found it increasingly difficult to form families. Enslaved Africans started to revolt in the United States and in other countries. The law denied the right to marry to all African people who were enslaved in the United Sates (Hallam, 2018). However the agricultural demands of this barbaric slave-minded society continued to generate a disproportionate population of enslaved African men, further restricting African men and women from being intimate.

Although African men and women naturally continued to desire comfort from one another, the evil-doers in power were only concerned about how the large number of African men to women potentially posed a threat of revolution. This fear is historically a part of where the Second Amendment, "Right to Bear Arms", came from in 1789-1791.

Since America was newly formed after a bloody revolution from Britain, the United States government did not allow all of its citizens to keep weapons in their homes out of fear that they would overthrow the government. However, those same citizens were required by law to help catch a slave if they ran away. To address the citizens growing fear of African men and the governments fear of another revolution in America, policy makers decided that allowing enslaved Africans to marry would make slaves content and less likely to revolt. With this in mind, we will continue to refer to Black men being intimately connected to Black women as a revolutionary act.

To thwart this revolution of Black people, policy makers

reasoned that marriage would make enslaved African people very docile, because most humans are content, happy and otherwise satisfied, when they are allowed to be with the ones they love and have created children with. The cruelties of capitalism continued to govern policies of marital relationships for the enslaved.

Slave-owners further rationalized that allowing the enslaved Africans to marry would lead to reliable reproduction cycles and ultimately be more lucrative for their overall bottom line financially. The idea of a self-renewing labor force was exploited on a grand scale for the first time on plantations of late 18th century America (Hallam, 2018). Even after slavery ended, governmental separation of African American men and women was deliberate and intentional.

The cruelties of capitalism continued to make it difficult for enslaved Africans to experience true intimacy in their relationships. Decades and decades of research on Black love suggest that African Americans were not afforded the same capitalist freedoms as White Americans, and a breakdown of intimacy between Black men and women continued to occur (Anderson & Mealy, 1979; Franklin, (1984); Bell, Bouie, & Baldwin, 1990; Taylor & McClain, 1997).

Researchers agree that this breakdown in intimacy occurred, because of the inability of Black men to adequately provide for their families. Innately, most men consider the ability to provide for their families the basic principle of manhood. Consider a few of the realities of discrimination that African American men have faced since the end of forced slavery: the lack of access to capital, lack of access to buying land, lack of rights to retain land, lack of access to the industrialized labor force, lack of access to adequate healthcare, and essentially the lack of the ability to defend and protect the Black woman and economically provide for their families. As a result. Black men saw themselves as failures, leaving the family building responsibility to Black women (Taylor & McClain, 1997). A Black woman's need to voice her frustration and a Black man's need to feel powerful stems from this animosity that was caused by the ills of forced slavery and unregulated capitalism that has gone unrecognized and untreated.

The perspective on how we move to a deeper commitment to love each other, whether in romantic relationships, business relationships or family relationships is different in various bodies of research. For the purpose of this discussion on intimacy, we will look at choosing to focus on your spouse's *needs* as the ultimate act of intimacy and meaningful connection.

To begin that discussion we must delve into a clear definition on what trauma is. We must also examine the lingering effects of the trauma of our enslaved ancestors, as well as the trauma of our spouses. Of course, we will look at our personal trauma: what we have experienced and continue to endure in everyday life. Trauma, especially when it is untreated can affect our relationships and our capacity to receive and provide intimacy.

Troya Bishop, M.Ed.

CHAPTER ONE – ACTION GUIDE
THE HISTORY OF BROKEN INTIMACY IN MY FAMILY

African men, women and children being separated is painful. Equally as painful is the separation of marriages and relationships in *your* family. Reflect back as far as you can and on relationships in your family. Who got married? What was their love story? How did they stay together? Why did it end? I encourage you to ask these questions to people in your life from your mother's family and your father's family.

My Mother and Father – Their Story of Love

1. When did they meet? How old were they?

   _____

   _____

2.   What was their love story? Who initiated the relationship?

_____

_____

3.   What types of activities did they do for fun?

_____

4.   How long did they stay together?

_____

_____

5.   What strategies did they use to maintain their relationship OR

Why did they choose to separate? Was it a peaceful

separation?

_____

_____

_____

6.   How have you seen them relate to one another?

_____

_____

7.   How does their affection for each other or the lack thereof

make you feel?

_____

8. How has your observation of your parents affected your relationships?

_____

_____

9. How has your parents relationships affected your siblings relationships?

_____

_____

10. How did your parents relationship develop or change as you got older?

_____

_____

11. Did you see kindness and intimacy in your home when you were growing-up?

_____

_____

12. How did all of the factors in questions 1-11 effect your past and current relationships?

_____

CHAPTER TWO
TRAUMA IS REAL

What is trauma? According to the American Psychological Association (APA), **trauma** is an emotional response to an awful and unexpected event (2018). Doctors with the APA suggest that immediately after a traumatic event, a person will usually have feelings of shock and denial. They also suggest that long term responses to a traumatic experience can include unpredictable emotions, flashbacks, strained relationships and even physical symptoms like headaches or nausea (APA, 2018). According to leading psychologist and national talk show host, Dr. Phil McGraw, the lasting effects of the stress from a traumatic event can become a chronic disorder if it goes untreated. This condition is most often referred to as post-traumatic stress disorder.

Dr. Phil's definition of **Post-Traumatic Stress Disorder (PTSD)** is, "a complex anxiety disorder that may develop after exposure to an extremely stressful or life-threatening event — involving death, the threat of death or serious injury — with resulting intense fear, helplessness or horror" (McGraw, 2018). However, many Black people, African American people, and other people of color in America experience traumatic events, rooted in racism, on a daily consistent basis.

This type of trauma is called **constant traumatic stress** (Bishop, 2016). As concretely established in, *The Answers: Discussing and Defeating Racism in America*, when you consider the hundreds of ways and thousands of places where racist experiences take place and can cause trauma, it is easy to understand why constant traumatic stress is present in the life of many Black people, African American people, and other people of color. Certified personal trainer and fitness expert, Glenn Andrews, explains that constant traumatic stress shows up in all areas of the body. That's why African American people are often diagnosed with diseases that are rooted in stress. In order to maintain optimal body function and avoid chronic illnesses the stress must be addressed on a daily basis when working out and training the muscles to relieve stress and trauma (Andrews, 2016). However, most people with constant traumatic stress do not address the stress in their lives in healthy ways. Not with physical activity or psychological treatment. Many people self-medicate with alcohol or marijuana. Most people normalize it.

To **normalize** means to recognize an experience as normal or typical to ease pain and anxiety. Through normalizing chaos that happens in daily activities, Black people may often minimize the reality of the trauma and the pain they experience (Ricks, 2018) which is a breeding ground for toxic behaviors that are further barriers to intimacy. Those barriers are the same as the effects of trauma discussed earlier: withdrawal, depression, self-medicating, impulsivity, anger, anxiety, etc. To achieve intimacy in a relationship, these barriers caused by trauma must be eliminated. The best way to eliminate the barriers to intimacy is through counseling and intentional therapy.

Most people will acknowledge the stigma in the Black community against seeking counseling for feelings of sadness, anger, rage, and depression. Many Black people, and other people of color, fear seeking counseling due to the fear of rejection and fear of isolation if someone believes you to be *crazy*. I also believe the stigma of seeking counseling in communities of color is deeply rooted in the pain of racism.

Some non-Black people have insisted for years that slavery was not that bad, and have also recently insisted that racism was over. Under the Obama Presidential Administration, many journalists, researchers and news correspondents urged those of us in the social justice community to say that we were in a post-racial era. Now that a new administration is in the White House, the conversations about racism being, "over", have come to a deafening silent halt.

Perhaps Black people do not choose to further subject themselves to people who will not believe their experiences, like those journalists and news correspondents. Experiencing trauma is painful, but if someone shares that pain with the intention of getting help and they are judged and shunned, the trauma and lasting effects are exacerbated. Or perhaps Black people have seen someone being killed by the police on camera with clear visual and audio proof, and many people *still* do not believe that an injustice occurred. With this in mind, let us resolve to encourage those who have experienced trauma to get help. When we speak about a person's reluctance to seek counsel, our words should be reassuring and encouraging. Condescending comments about someone's reluctance to seek help is completely unacceptable.

Many people of various ethnic groups who have experienced trauma are also experiencing difficulty with being in loving relationships (romantic, family and platonic) and are not aware that they have untreated trauma. Due to the severity of the unacknowledged and untreated trauma, many wonderful well-intentioned people are not able to function in a healthy loving way toward another person in a relationship. In order to get deeper into intimacy, we must embrace the redefinition of trauma, which we have established is a barrier to intimacy.

Researcher and Old Dominion University professor, Dr. Shawn Ricks, insists that trauma must be redefined (2018). Many Black and African American women and men have normalized the constant traumatic stress in their lives and use the general APA definition of trauma which does not consider the Black experience or the experiences of other people of color. In addition to microaggressions from racism, Dr. Ricks suggests that traumatic experiences for women can also include fighting consistently to have your voice heard, fighting for your child's psychological development, hoping no one sees your fears, and putting on "the mask" of strength to carry the mantle of being a Strong Black Woman (SBW). Including more experiences that Black people face daily will help Black couples have more understanding of each other's wounds and needs to achieve deeper intimacy.

Being aware of the trauma each partner brings into a relationship is paramount with achieving intimacy. Jada Pinkett Smith, host of the hit web series *Red Table Talk*, also suggests that most people come into relationships with a plethora of traumatic experiences and expectations of the other person that are far too high (Smith, 2018).

"Traumas and expectations can be a painful mix because it's our traumas and the false beliefs they create, that keep us from offering our best to ourselves and to others. We are all a bunch of open wounds slamming into each other all day, every day. Successful relating is not for the weak at heart. This is why I believe relationships are a spiritual endeavor". – Jada Pinkett Smith

In order to set healthy expectations for our relationships and limit the effects of trauma, we must clearly define what intimacy is and what it should look like in a healthy relationship. We must also differentiate between sexual intimacy and non-sexual intimacy, to equip couples who want to love each other in a genuine way with the tool to do so.

Troya Bishop, M.Ed.

CHAPTER TWO – ACTION GUIDE
YOUR TRAUMA IS REAL

Trauma can deeply effect your life and your relationships. Reflect over your life and consider where you may have experienced trauma. After the event did you experience deep feelings of anger, shock and/or denial? Were you provided with treatment? Did you respond to trauma with any of these symptoms: unpredictable emotions, flashbacks, strained relationships, headaches or nausea?

Age 3-6 years old?

_____

_____

Age 7-10 years old?

_____

_____

Age 11-14 years old?

_____

_____

Age 15-18 years?

_____

_____

Age 20-30 years old?

_____

_____

Age 30-40 years old?

_____

_____

The lasting effects of the stress from a traumatic event can become a **chronic disorder** if it goes untreated. This condition is most often referred to as **post-traumatic stress disorder. Constant traumatic stress** is when you experience traumatic events like microaggressions on a consistent, daily basis.

Do you experience trauma on a daily basis?

_____

What or who is causing the constant traumatic stress?

_____

_____

How do you handle to stress or trauma in your life?

_____

_____

Have you normalized the trauma in your life?

_____

_____

If the trauma you experienced as a child has affected your ability to have a relationship or work to earn a living on a consistent basis, you may have post-traumatic stress disorder. Please use your writings from this book to share with your physician, your clinician, or someone you love. You may need additional support and direct counseling to overcome the trauma you experienced. Be sure to find a provider that is culturally competent and empathetic to YOUR CULTURE and ethnic background to assure the best care possible.

Effects of trauma can also manifest in your life as barriers to intimacy: withdrawal, depression, self-medicating, impulsivity, anger, anxiety, etc.

Have you been in a relationship with someone who suggested that you display some of these barriers? Which symptoms?

_____

_____

_____

Have these barriers affected you in other relationships that are not romantic? Like with friends, family, co-workers, fraternity members, etc.? In which relationships?

_____

_____

_____

If you answered yes to any of the above questions, share your responses with a trusted friend, and talk through your feelings. It may be a good time for you to seek additional support and counsel from a mental health care provider in your area. Choose a provider that is culturally competent and empathetic to YOUR CULTURE and ethnic background to assure the best care possible.

Dr. Shawn Ricks, a leading researcher on African American women, suggests that traumatic experiences can also include fighting consistently to have your voice heard, fighting for your child's psychological development, hoping no one sees your fears, and putting on "the mask" of strength to carry the mantle of being a Strong Black Woman (SBW).

1. Do you identify as a SBW? Why/ Why not?

2. Are you consistently fighting for your voice to be heard in your relationship? In your family? At your job? In society?

3. Do you wear the mask of strength to hide your fears? Why/ Why not?

_____

_____

_____

_____

4. Do you have to fight for your child's psychological

    development? Why? If so, what does that fight include?

    _____

    _____

    _____

    _____

    If you answered yes to any of the above questions, you may

    be experiencing trauma. Please use your writings from this

    book to share with your physician, your clinician, or someone

    you love. You may need additional support and direct

    counseling to overcome the trauma you experienced. Be sure

    to find a provider that is culturally competent and empathetic

    to YOUR CULTURE and ethnic background to assure the

    best care possible.

CHAPTER THREE
THE BEAUTY OF INTIMACY

What is intimacy? **Intimacy** is an interactive process that involves sharing, receiving and knowing about the deepest most secret, inner aspects of another person. It is also an essential factor in the interpersonal relationships of everyday life, as well as a core component of our spiritual relationship with God (Holland, Lee, Marshak, & Martin 2016). Intimacy and closeness with someone you love and who loves you in return is truly beautiful. With this in mind, we must explore intimacy in romantic relationships.

Intimacy in a relationship is complex and depends on several things. The depth of intimacy depends on a person's perception of the intimate relationship and the depth of communication in that relationship. Feeling safe when you are being vulnerable with your partner and feeling safe during times of conflict are important components of intimacy (Holland et al, 2016). Research suggests that how your partner responds to you is important to feeling safe and is related to greater openness and emotional risk-taking especially when the result of your openness is potentially undesirable. **Commitment** and faithfulness are also key factors for feeling safe in a relationship.

Commitment makes a person feel safe and is the most powerful and consistent predictor of marital satisfaction (Holland et al, 2016). Since we now know that commitment and faithfulness are keys to deeper intimacy, why do people choose to go wider in intimate relationships, instead of deeper, when intimacy is what people crave?

For example, many people will pull back when they feel they are falling in love. Others will seek other partners for immediate sexual closeness and have multiple sexual partners or multiple relationships, instead of exploring the deeper intimacy of the person they are currently married to or involved with. I call it *going wider* in relationships and intimacy, instead of *going deeper*. People do this based on a real fear of intimacy that is rooted in trauma. Perhaps the trauma is in genetic memory of the pain of slavery and separation of men from women and their children. Perhaps that trauma stems from a previous divorce or death of a loved one.

We know that trauma is a barrier to intimacy, and can last for several generations in your DNA if it is not addressed. Research has shown that the behavioral effects of trauma can be passed down to the next generation with trauma's negative effects (Schwartz, 2014). As such, we should also understand that the trauma of separation can cause a fear of intimacy for many people in romantic relationships.

With that in mind, we must maintain a commitment to develop intimacy with those who have committed to us and remain committed to building a world of people who are loving and kind. To do that let's differentiate between sexual intimacy and non-sexual intimacy.

Dr. Bonnie Wright from the Honor Society of Nursing explains that **sexual intimacy** is a deep sense of knowing, understanding, belonging and connecting in spirit, during sexual intercourse. However, you can have sex with someone and not be intimate. This popular habit can become an addiction that does not get you closer to real intimacy. According to leading psychotherapist, Jack Daniels, sex is a drug so you have to be careful with it.

Oxytocin is a peptide hormone and neuropeptide produced in the brain during sex (Daniels, 2016). It is the bonding agent that connects you to the person you are having sex with. The more sex you have with a person, the more chemicals are released during, sex deepening the bond. This is the science behind sexual intimacy and bonding. However, Jack Daniels and other relationship experts urge couples to wait for sex until marriage, so that they can develop substance. Substance in a relationship is built with non-sexual intimacy.

Non-sexual intimacy, is more difficult to achieve than sexual intimacy and involves more of who you are than sexual ability (Wright, 2018). You can have an intimate relationship without having a sexual relationship. There are three main categories of non-sexual intimacy: sharing, being kind, and giving.

Couples developing an intimate relationship can share meaningful activities that you can both relate to and therefore relate more deeply to each other (Wright, 2018). Those activities may include art, music, or reading a book to each other. Any activity that "shares" a part of who you are, is sharing. Sharing a special song that you refer to as, *your song*, is also a non-sexual way of being intimate. Whenever you hear it played no matter where you are, the song's meaning is a bond you share with each other, even if you are surrounded by thousands of people at a concert. Kindness is also a general category for non-sexual intimacy.

Being kind may be a common gesture but that gesture may have meaning to you because it demonstrates the consistent respect and care you have for each other. It could be as simple as opening a door for your spouse or helping them put on their coat. Sharing can also be completing a chore they usually do, to show that you understand and appreciate all they do for you. Giving is also important in building intimacy in any relationship.

Giving of yourself and your time fearlessly can include taking a walk in the park, giving them their favorite food or drink or going to church. We will go deeper into giving and the deeper meaning behind gift giving that helps you to bond as we go in-depth into the 5 Love Languages in Chapter 7. Developing a balance between sexual and non-sexual intimacy is important for maintaining psychological health and a healthy relationship in general.

Psychological health does not mean that you always experience positive emotions and maintain intimacy with your relationship partners. Nor does it mean that you don't feel emotional pain. What it does mean is that you can step in and out of these emotional states when you need to. You might even do it with ease, with enough practice.   This ability is the root system for emotional intelligence.

CHAPTER THREE – ACTION GUIDE
THE BEAUTY OF YOUR INTIMACY

Non-sexual intimacy builds substance and longevity in relationships. Talk to your spouse about your ideas on non-sexual intimacy. Create a "bucket list" of the top ways you would like to explore non-sexual intimacy with your partner. Here are a few additional suggestions from *Thought Catalog*:

1. Give each other a ten-minute massage before bed.

2. Sit in a park on a shared towel so you're forced to cozy up.

3. Send a flirtatious text message that builds anticipation, or one that just lets your partner know you're thinking about him/her.

4. Reminisce about your first date or the first time you slept together.

5. Cook dinner together while dancing to music around the kitchen.

6. Put on "your song" and spend the entire length of the song uninterrupted, staring into each other's eyes without talking. Then reflect on the experience.

9. Exercise together — couples who sweat together stay together.

10. Every night, express gratitude for one thing your partner did that day — no matter how small the act (examples are doing the dishes, grocery shopping, sending a loving text, planning a vacation, a kiss goodbye that morning).   ***Continue with your list here***

11._____

12._____

13. _____

14. _____

15._____

16. _____

17._____

18._____

19._____

20._____

CHAPTER FOUR
EMOTIONAL INTELLIGENCE

According to leading psychology journal, *Psychology Today*, **emotional intelligence** (EI) is evident when a person is: 1) aware of their emotional state 2) able to manage their emotional state, 3) aware of other people's emotional state, and 4) able to effectively manage their response to other people's emotional state (2015). Being aware of your emotions is the beginning of developing emotional intelligence.

Emotional intelligence first requires us to discover and nurture an **inner awareness** of our thoughts and our feelings (Goleman, 2013). Inner awareness is when you are present and awake in your own mind, body and soul to examine and understand what you feel. Developing emotional intelligence requires applying that inner awareness in managing your upsets and focusing on your goals.

Understanding what you feel and why you are having those feelings is key in developing EI. Many dietitians use journaling to help their clients understand what emotions are triggering their emotional eating. They will also ask the clients to keep a track of what they are doing to accomplish their goals and what they need to do to remain focused on their goals. In that same vein, some surgeons refuse to do bariatric surgery and other major weight-loss surgeries without the long-term counsel of a psychologist to help the patient determine the emotional causes of their weight gain. When you understand what you feel, you can find resources and strategies to help you effectively address those emotions. Developing EI also requires a focus on others.

Raising your emotional intelligence level requires an intentional connection to other people, especially your spouse. This connection is also where intimacy lives. Your relationship thrives, when you focus on how to relate to them, how to understand them and how to have effective interactions with them based on that intentional focus (Goleman, 2013). With that in mind, your response to them and their needs will also be rooted in emotional intelligence.

When you have emotional intelligence as the base from where you respond to your spouse's needs, meeting their needs is not as stressful because you share their perspective.

CHAPTER FOUR – ACTION GUIDE
EMOTIONAL INTELLIGENCE

A healthy level of emotional intelligence is necessary to develop intimacy in a relationship. Take a few moments to reflect on your emotional intelligence.

Are you aware of your emotional state?

_____

_____

When your emotional state changes, how do you handle it?

_____

_____

Are you aware of your spouse's emotional state?

_____

_____

How do you respond to fluctuations in your spouse's emotional state?

_____

_____

A practice that some people use to awaken their inner awareness is called **centering**. Centering is grounding yourself in the present moment and being fully engaged with the task at hand. Remaining centered helps you manage disappointment and focus on your goals. What are some long term goals for your life that you can center on to help you manage disappointment?

_____

_____

_____

_____

_____

What are some long term goals for your relationship that you can center on to help you manage disappointment?

_____

_____

_____

_____

_____

Use your favorite search engine to find emotional intelligence tests to determine your score and find strategies to improve your score.

CHAPTER FIVE
THE ART OF LISTENING

Your perspective on what it means to listen is also very important when creating intimacy with someone you love. Think about it: how many times have you been told that you don't listen? Now, consider how many times you have actually been *taught* to listen. Did you have a lesson on listening in elementary school? Middle School? High School? College? At work? At church? At the doctor's office? Yet, how well you listen affects you in every area of your life, especially your physical health. Now compare: how many times you have been *told* that you don't listen to how many times you have been *taught* to listen. It's no wonder that you are not the best at listening. However, you are not alone.

Most people do not listen well. Maybe that is exactly why statistics show that most relationships i.e. romantic relationships, family relationships, friendships and even business relationships end because of complications in communicating. We know how to talk. That is not the problem. The problem is that we do not know *how* to listen. Before we learn *how* to listen, we must clearly define *what* listening is. There are two basic types of listening: passive listening and active listening.

Passive listening is paying attention in order to hear something (Nemec, Spagnolo, & Soydan, 2018). That is what most people do, and is why people tell you, "you are NOT listening". **Active listening** includes compassionate and empathic responses, as well as words and actions. It is based on the listener being able to see the perspective of the other person from their point of view (Nemec et al, 2018). Active listening also includes being able to sense how the speaker is feeling. It includes a full skill set.

Before we discuss the skill set active listening includes, let us be clear: active listening does *not* include judgement or the listener's feelings on the content that the speaker is talking about. Judgment is detrimental to any conversation. When a person passes **judgement,** they form a condescending, concrete opinion about what they hear. Judgement may challenge the speaker's view, internally in the listeners mind or aloud, for the speaker to hear (Nemec et al, 2018). The listener's feelings are also not a part of active listening. Although this may sound a bit harsh, the danger in the listener including *their* feelings in what they hear, is that they may imagine how *they* would feel instead of how the speaker feels. Remember, listening is always about the speaker. Not about the listener. In the context of constant traumatic stress, this is hard to achieve, yet it is necessary in order to have deeper intimacy and effective communication. Now that we clearly understand what active listening *is not*, we will look definitively at what active listening is.

Authentic **active listening** is a set of skills that require a listener to practice intentional integration of the components of active listening into a conversation. The components of active listening are: preparing to listen, asking open-ended questions, paraphrasing and reflective listening (Nemec et al, 2018). Preparing to listen is the most important element of active listening.

Mental preparation is needed for continuous and attentive listening (McClelland, 2018). Good listeners are ready to take in *everything* that the speaker is saying. Preparing to listen also requires setting aside other tasks (not multi-tasking), attending to physical needs (like kids or your cell phone), centering yourself, and becoming oriented to the upcoming conversation. After properly preparing yourself to listen, you should then be ready to respond to the speaker with compassion and open-ended questions.

Open-ended questions show you are truly listening, because you are requesting additional information from the speaker. These questions deepen the conversation by highlighting an unstructured question in which possible answers (like multiple choice) are not suggested (Business Dictionary, 2018). Open-ended questions let the other person in the conversation know there is no judgement. The respondent is able to answer in his or her own words. Open-ended questions typically begin with: how, what, when, where, or why. In addition to using open-ended questions to deepen the understanding of what the speaker is saying, another component of active listening is paraphrasing.

Paraphrasing is restating what you heard the speaker say, using different words. For example, someone paraphrasing may use the words, "What I heard you say is..." or " I believe you are sharing that…". To fully clarify the speakers' meaning without using judgment, the listener restates the facts. Paraphrasing communicates understanding and lets the other person in the conversation know that you are listening carefully (McClelland, 2018). Active listening also requires that the listener is compassionate with the speaker and that they reflect empathetic feelings when listening.

Reflecting feelings is also referred to as **vulnerable listening**, and it captures the feelings associated with the speaker's experiences. Reflective feelings or vulnerable listening include: emotional dangers associated with listening, non-verbal communication of the listener's body, and the role of extreme emotions in, such as feeling outraged or embarrassed. Researcher Sara McClelland from the University of Michigan admits that with all of this in mind, one must admit that listening is a difficult skill that takes practice and comes with possibilities as well as challenges (2017). Considering all of the components of listening, think about the challenges a person with untreated constant traumatic stress will endure while trying to listen. We must continue to listen and love with the intention to understand, share compassion and enhance intimacy.

In order to enhance intimacy, we must learn to use active listening.

We must listen with compassion, listen with the intention to understand, and listen with the intention to connect deeply. It took me a while to even understand the concept of listening with compassion.

Like so many other people, I thought that listening and *not talking* were the same things. If somebody told me they felt like I was not listening, I would simply take a deep breath and stop talking. I was wrong. That is not listening with compassion. It is hearing, or passive listening. Relationship coach, Renee Wade, suggests that listening with compassion is caring enough about the person speaking to switch into compassionate mode (Wade, 2018).

She also suggests that when we say we want to be listened to, we are asking the person we are speaking to for compassion to be shown towards us. As such, Wade coined the word, "compassioning", as a more appropriate term for listening with compassion (2018). Listening with compassion also means that you refuse to defend your position, and put yourself in a deep place of compassion toward the other person.

Since 85% of what we communicate is nonverbal, the other person can easily determine if you are being compassionate toward them based on your eye movement, arm position, mouth position, head movement and other body language. If you are defending your position you probably are not listening with compassion. Listening with compassion will help us to understand the perspective of the speaker. The final and perhaps most crucial component in compassionate listening is refusing to be offended.

Offended means, upset by an annoyance or resentment brought about by a perceived insult to or disregard for oneself or one's standards or principles (Merriam-Webster, 2018). My journey to understanding the power of not being offended has been interesting. At the end of every year I use my private time with God to ask Him what I need to work on to develop spiritually. In 2014, He was very clear that I needed to work on not being offended. I did not understand why I should be concerned with it. After all, it was THEM who did something to ME. Why should I be concerned?

We should be concerned and remain in love and in compassion at all times if we are going to develop meaningful relationships with business partners and family members and deeper intimacy with our spouse. Keep in mind that most people are thinking about themselves. So they didn't attend a meeting or party to get there to offend you. It is not about you. It is about them and their perspective. If we choose to love them enough to have compassion for them, and look at things from their perspective there is no room for offense.

Yes, this sounds simple but is very hard to accomplish. Like everything else that we do well, choosing compassion over offense takes a lot of time, maturity and practice. To begin practicing not being easily offended, we must understand perspective. Perspective is key in developing deeper intimacy.

CHAPTER FIVE – ACTION GUIDE
THE ART OF YOUR LISTENING

Before reading the chapter on listening, were you a good listener?

Why/Why not?

_____

_____

_____

_____

_____

After reading the chapter on listening, what are some ways you can

improve as a listener?

_____

_____

_____

How can being a better listener improver intimacy in your relationship?

_____

_____

_____

We established what it means to be offended. Do you get offended often? Why/Why not?

_____

_____

_____

How will it benefit your business relationships and your mental health by choosing not to be offended? With your boss? With your co-workers?

_____

_____

_____

_____

_____

_____

_____

How will it benefit your family relationships by choosing not to be offended? With your siblings? With your parents? With your children?

_____

_____

_____

_____

How will it deepen intimacy in your relationship with your spouse by choosing not to be offended?

_____

_____

_____

_____

_____

_____

_____

_____

_____

CHAPTER SIX
THE POWER OF PERSPECTIVE

The Cambridge Dictionary defines **perspective** as a particular way of viewing things that depends on a person's experience and personality (2018). Your perspective on your power, being *powerful vs* being *powerless*, manifests itself in the way we express our sexuality with our spouse or partners. Before we examine the relationship between power and sexuality, let's look more closely at the social construct of power.

Power is possession-of-control, having authority, or possessing total influence over others (Merriam-Webster, 2018). As we established earlier, we live in a system that is constructed to specifically remove power from a particular group of people. Those people that are socially engineered to be powerless in American society are African American men and women, other people of color, and women (Bishop, 2016). Regardless of how powerful of a position an African American or Black man has, there is always a White person who can somehow undermine that power.

President Obama and his administration are a perfect example of that principle. During his presidency he was the most powerful person in the world in theory and on paper. However, because he was Black, the social construct of racism rendered him powerless in many ways. Many racists publically and proudly shared that their number one goal as an elected official (or person with power) was to make sure President Obama failed. With that in mind, consider the power or lack thereof, for the average Black man working in his job or career.

Although Black men and African American men may have a powerful position as a pastor, a congressman, lawyer, principal, or entertainer; in a hostile racist society he may still feel powerless. We established that power directly refers to the possession of control over something; being able to effect the outcome of something.

There are many instances of police murder, judicial misconduct, improprieties in school systems through the school-to-prison pipeline that men have no perceived power to change or control. They do not have immediate power to change or control those injustices although they have the power to participate in the process of change, as many of them do. Due to the systemic oppression of racism, many men, especially Black men are rendered powerless. The perception of power is important.

Again, if a man's priority is to provide safety and economic stability for his family and he is unable to give them that, where can he receive a sense of power? From his perspective, perhaps the only other place he can feel powerful in a safe and healthy way is in his bedroom through his psyche.

The basic reasons men love receiving oral sex is because it gives them: 1) a deep feeling of power, 2) a feeling of domination, and 3) a fulfilled need to sense someone else's vulnerability. Feeling powerful is necessary in order for a man to feel masculine. This feeling can be difficult for some men to accomplish in an overtly racist and oppressive society. According to relationship expert, Renee Wade, oral sex is also a healthy way for men to access the power of their dark masculine energy (Wade, 2018).

This masculine energy is akin to a deep animalistic desire to feel powerful and is innate in most men, regardless of ethnic background. Many scientists, psychologists and relationship experts also suggest that not expressing the need to feel powerful in a healthy sexual way can be the root of a sexual and social disconnection. There is a plethora of research in psychology that suggests that rape and child molestation are not about sex, but about the abuse of power. Those gruesome, violent acts are a perverted way for predators to fulfill a psychological need to feel powerful and to dominate. They also receive vulnerability and innocence from their victim.

To **dominate** means to have control over a place or a person, or to be the most important person or thing (Cambridge English Dictionary, 2018). Cultures in other countries appreciate competition, but in some sub-cultures in the United States, some obsess with their ability to dominate. Whether it is a sports team, a favorite show or a political affiliation, some obsess with being *the* best instead of being *their* best. This philosophy is rooted in masculine energy and the need to dominate.

Similarly, Renee Wade suggests in her international relationship series *The Feminine Woman*, that some men desire to feel like he has the freedom to dominate his woman every now and then. Even the *gentlemen* who try not to own their dark side have a profound desire to dominate because it is innate in their masculine energy. In her articles and in her coaching, she urges men not to reject the, "dark side" (2018). When you reject the need to dominate, it becomes an obsession. Over time, the dark side manifests itself in our lives in twisted, pathological ways that hurt other people. The release of the dark side is one reason men love oral sex. However, men also love oral sex to release their need to feel someone is vulnerable and submitted to them.

Vulnerability is a requirement for intimacy to be firmly established in a relationship. To be **vulnerable** is able to be willing to be effortlessly physically, emotionally, or mentally hurt, influenced, or attacked (Cambridge English Dictionary, 2018). We can use the word submission synonymously. Many of us have been exposed to the word submission in a spiritual context, of humility and servitude in marriage. However, it is also appropriate to use it in a sexual context as is related to intimacy in a relationship.

From a physical perspective, consider the most submissive position that a woman can assume with her husband. Perhaps it is the position of the couple facing each other and the woman kneeling in front of him.   To form an intimate sexual connection, and to exchange feminine and masculine energy, vulnerability must take place. This submission and vulnerability of oral sex gives the man multiple feelings of amazement through the ecstatic attraction from the view of submission, psychological pleasure of being dominate, and of course the physical pleasure. In most circumstances, women enjoy sex as much as men do. But the purpose of this book is to discuss and contrast the deeply innate and intimate NEEDS of men and women. Not sexual differences or sexual preferences.

From the perspective of many women, an ultimate source of pleasure is being able to freely share her thoughts and concerns without judgement or correction, and knowing that she is being listened to, fully heard and completely understood. Whether it is telling a person at work exactly how she feels about their behavior or speaking to her significant other about what transpired during the day, a woman needs to be heard. Creating the space in a relationship for a woman to freely speak about what is on her mind will open the pathway for a man to get exactly what he needs in a relationship.

When she can come to a partner and to a space where she can release everything inside of her mind and her spirit, she has room to take in her spouse physically to give him what he needs. Any time before that point, she does not have room to take him in. Literally. She has to get everything out, before she can take more in. She has to know that her partner wants to hear her thoughts and is listening to her. This takes a lot of vulnerability on the man's part. To be open to listening without judging, fixing or correcting.

Just like the man wants to know that his partner is enjoying pleasing him sexually a woman needs to know that a man is engaged in the listening process. Both partners must create space to be vulnerable in order for the needs of their partner to be met. Vulnerability can be scary for both partners, especially when there has been hurt, abuse or abandonment in past relationships with family members or other intimate partners.

The concept of vulnerability goes hand-in-hand with the idea of trust. Men and women share a need to be trusted. When you are comfortable being fully vulnerable to each other, this indicates that you have established a firm foundation of trust. This exchange sounds simple but like anything else that we do well, it will take time, maturity and practice. We will go into more graphic detail in, *The Answer Parties*, so be sure to visit the website for updates on events near you.

CHAPTER SIX – ACTION GUIDE
THE POWER OF YOUR PERSPECTIVE

We have established **perspective** as a particular way of viewing things that depends on a person's experience and personality and **power** is possession-of-control, having authority, or possessing total influence over others. Let's take a look from your perspective.

On a scale from 1 to 10, with 1 meaning little power and 10 meaning an extreme amount of power, how powerful do you feel at work? At home? In your extended family? In your local community? In your national society? In the world?

_____

_____

_____

_____

_____

How does your power or lack of power make you feel? I.e. happy, excited, fearful, angry, uncertain, depressed, etc.?

_____

_____

_____

When and where can you express your need to feel powerful?

_____

_____

_____

When and where do you dominate?

_____

_____

_____

How does dominating make you feel?

_____

_____

_____

Vulnerability is a requirement for intimacy to be firmly established in a relationship. To be **vulnerable** is able to be willing to be effortlessly physically, emotionally, or mentally hurt, influenced, or attacked.

Have you demonstrated that you are willing to be vulnerable to your partner? How do you know?

_____

_____

_____

_____

What is the best way that your partner can be vulnerable to you?

_____

_____

_____

_____

What is your deepest need in your relationship?

_____

_____

_____

Use this space to write a note to your spouse, expressing to them what you need most from them? At home? For your career? Spiritually? Emotionally? Sexually? Mentally? Physically? Financially?

_____

_____

_____

_____

_____

_____

_____

_____

_____

_____

_____

_____

_____

_____

_____

_____

_____

CHAPTER SEVEN
THE FIVE LOVE LANGUAGES

There are many ways to express love. There are also many ways that people receive love and feel that they are indeed being loved by someone. The problem is, some people give love in a way that their partner does not interpret as love. For example, if spending time with someone equates love in your mind, but the person you are in relationship with shows you love through giving gifts, there can be love lost and trust broken in that relationship, even though both people have a genuine interest and desire to love each other. Fortunately, there is a solution to this problem.

In 1992 Dr. Gary Chapman published the book, *The Five Love Languages: How to Express Heartfelt Commitment to Your Mate*. Since then, this book has been #1 and in the top 5 on the New York Times bestsellers list. So I am certainly not the only one who believe it is an excellent resource on learning how to love. In the book, Dr. Chapman teaches that there are 5 love languages: quality time, receiving gifts, words of affirmation, physical touch and acts of service. Although you may be able to recognize your preferences in each of the love languages, most people have one distinct primary love language.

A husband and wife rarely have the same primary love language. We tend to speak our own language and wonder why our partner does not respond how we would like them to (Chapman, 2018). They did not get the message on an emotional level since it was not given in their love language. If you express your love by doing things for your spouse, but what they want is physical touch, the message of love and connection is lost. If your spouse gives you a gift, but what you really want is to go to dinner with them, the message of love and connection is lost. You are both sincere, but you are not connecting. Once you discover and speak your spouse's primary love language, real intimacy can be achieved.

Passionate love does not have to disappear after marriage or exclusive commitment. Most of us will have to learn a second language for intimacy and deep connection to become a real part of our relationship. We cannot simply do what comes naturally for us. We must learn to speak our partner's love language, and that takes intention and effort (Chapman, 2018). Don't worry. You can do it. We will begin with examining the top ways people feel loved: quality time and words of affirmation.

Spending time with someone doing things you know they enjoy is the love language of quality time. Often, a partner enjoys that time together even more, if they know the one they are with is making a sacrifice to do something they are not good at or typically do not enjoy. For example, if your spouse's love language is quality time and they love musicals, but you have a busy schedule and hate musicals, they would really appreciate you taking time to go to a musical with them. It can be easy to love our partners in their love language with thought and effort. Using kind words to show love is also one of the most prevalent love languages.

Some people particularly enjoy hearing verbal praise when they do well and hearing kinds words that reassure them that they are loved. Keep in mind that these people are also effected in a greater way by criticism and arguing, because words mean more to them than to people who do not have words of affirmation as their primary love language. Acts of service is another way people receive love.

Having someone to do things to help relieve some responsibility and stress is an act of service. A person whose primary love language is acts of service is one who you have heard say, "actions speak louder than words". According to the 5 Love Languages website, many people who have acts of service as a primary love language often have receiving gifts as a secondary love language (2018). Receiving gifts does not mean that your partner is superficial.

It simply means that like acts of service, they enjoy a gesture of your love. Knowing what your partner likes and how they like to receive gifts is also important to discover as you deepen intimacy. The last love language is the one many people equate with intimacy; physical touch.

Physical touch can be a difficult love language, because there can be some uncertainty around knowing when it is appropriate to touch. People who have physical touch as their primary love language often have quality time as a secondary love language. However, there is some overlap in all of the love languages. Being willing to express your love in as many ways as possible to connect more deeply with your partner is essential in building intimacy.

All people want to be loved unconditionally. A child longs for this kind of love from their parents, and husbands and wives also desire unconditional love from each other (Chapman, 2018). Unfortunately, too many people are waiting for their spouse to make the first move. We sit back and say, "When they decide to become affectionate, then I will… or when they decide to think about my needs, then I'll start loving them." These are examples of love with conditions. Someone has to take the lead in unconditional love. Why not you? Most spouses respond positively to unconditional love and relationships thrive on perceived reciprocity.

Perceived reciprocity has been described as a universal social norm concerning equity, balance, and fairness in relationships (Braun, Rohr, Wagner, & Kunzmann, 2018). Research suggests that a person's level of satisfaction in a relationships is related to how they perceive balance, shared responsibility and fairness in the relationship. Recent studies also show that couples who have balance and value in a relationship have longer lasting relationships.

CHAPTER SEVEN – ACTION GUIDE
FINDING YOUR LOVE LANGUAGES

Based on what you've read, what do you think your love language is?

_____

What do you think your spouse's love language is?

_____

Take the quiz at **5lovelanguages.com** to determine your primary

love language and then reflect. How is your quiz score different than

what you thought it would be? Discuss this with your partner.

_____

_____

How important is reciprocity in your relationship for you to feel satisfied, with 1 being not really important and 10 being extremely important?_____

Discuss this with your partner. Be sure to sign up for the weekly updates for tips on how to speak your partners love language at

5lovelanguages.com

CHAPTER EIGHT
LOVE NEVER ENDS
CONCLUSION

In 2008 I started on a journey of reading and research to uncover how racism can effect a person's life. I wrote a book that I never published, because it felt underdeveloped. I kept researching. As I reflect back on that time, I realize that the underdevelopment I felt was my personal inability to connect to my research on a deeper level of emotional commitment and intimacy.

I was deeply affected from the ugliness of racism and did not know how I should express it. I also was not aware that I needed to express it. Emotional trauma from racism and broken intimacy patterns in my family from divorce had stunted my emotional development and ability to connect deeply. My quest to heal and share my new knowledge about racism lead to a deeper understanding of love and relationships. Ultimately, conducting workshops, interacting with callers on radio shows, and hosting discussion sessions on social media lead me to connect the dots between racism, oppression and sexual expression and ntimacy.

Regardless of your spiritual practice, ethnic background or gender, we must be intentional with going deeper into intimacy in our relationships and not wider. More sexual partners is not the answer. I wholeheartedly believe that relationships suffer because people refuse to allow themselves to love deeply and trust completely. A deeper walk into intimacy can be scary, but vastly rewarding. Developing intimacy in relationships also helps us to grow, and ultimately reach our purpose as individuals and our collective purpose as a couple. That path to deep love and trust in a relationship is more difficult to accomplish for Black couples.

People who dare to love a Black or African American person is engaged in a revolutionary act, whether they realize it or not. In a society that has historic, consistent and prevalent reminders that the overarching belief of the governmental power structure is that Black and African American people should be mistreated, choosing to love a Black person is a direct action against that racist power structure. With that in mind, Black couples must find a way to do more healing, be more patient and be more intentional with how we interact with one another.

This applies to intimate relationships, as well as business and social relationships with Black people and African American people. We must find ways to remind Black men that they are powerful. We must find more ways to remind Black women that they are heard, and that their voices and experiences matter. Uplifting Black men and women will benefit all society members, because Black people created and continue to create the culture of the country.

Deeper intimacy in relationships will yield stable families, stable communities, cities and countries. Although where we are historically with broken intimacy is not our fault, it is our responsibility to educate ourselves, heal with intention, and create a better legacy for all who follow. When we commit to real intimacy, everyone wins. Committing to intimacy also means being willing to look at things from the perspective of the one you love.

Shared perspective helps you to be empathetic for those you love.

It supports you in being God-like, and practicing the omnipresence – which is looking at things from multiple perspectives at the same time. Seeing situations through the lens of _**your partner**_ will help you to find enough compassion to meet their needs. In a relationship, we must observe and listen to our lover's pain, oppression, or traumatic experience. Whether that need is a deeply primal sexual need of a man, or the need of a woman to verbally release and express herself. Having that need satisfied should be the goal of each partner in a deeply intimate couple.

Specific needs of every man and woman will vary. Needs of each couple will also vary. As such, it is paramount for both people in that relationship to ask what the needs are and to listen to each other. Listening seems like it would be synonymous with hearing, but it is not. Listening includes a set of skills that requires forethought and practice.

Active listening is compassionate and is based on the listener being able to see the perspective of the other person and sense how the speaker is feeling. It includes a full skill set. The listener should respond with: open-ended questions, paraphrasing, reflecting the speaker's feelings, and again with compassion. Listening with compassion also means that you refuse to defend your position, and put yourself in a profound place of compassion toward the other person. Refuse to be offended. Are you ready to get *that* intimate? Developing your emotional intelligence skills will help you to cultivate a more profound level of intimacy.

Emotional intelligence will give you the tools you need to listen address trauma and shift perspectives. As you develop your emotional intelligence, you will also simultaneously discover ways of speaking your partner's love language. When we speak in the love language of our partner and refuse to be offended, our relationships will grow deeper and more intimate. We must be willing to get outside of what is easy and comfortable to meet the needs of those we love. We must sacrifice and try things we never thought we would, spiritually physically, financially, and even sexually.

Sexual satisfaction is important. However, I want to be clear. I am not promoting promiscuity or casual sex. If you have experienced sexual abuse and are triggered by certain thoughts and activities, discuss that with your partner, be determined to heal and get help through a professional who is sensitive to your background and needs. I am promoting healthy, strong, committed and passionate relationships where there is intentional love and in some cases, revolutionary love. My prayer is that you will find a relationship that has all of those qualities. Grow in that relationship and nurture others through that relationship. Real revolution and political change starts at home, and that's what I'm all about.

Peace, Blessings, and Much Love

Troya Bishop, M.Ed.

RESOURCES

Note all of the references in this section were a part of the literature review for this book. They are not all used or cited in this work

American Psychological Association (2018). Definition of trauma. Retrieved from https://www.apa.org/topics/trauma/

Anderson, S.E., & Mealy, R. (1979). Who originated the crises? A historical perspective. *The Black Scholar*. 40-61.

Bell, Y.R.,, Bouie, C. L., & Baldwin, J.A., (1990). Afrocentric cultural consciousness and African-American male-female relationships. *Journal of Black Studies*. 1(2) 82-189.

Blomquist, B. A., & Giuliano, T. A. (2012). Do you love me, too? Perceptions of responses to I love you. *North American Journal of Psychology*, 14(2), 407–418. Retrieved from https://ezp.waldenulibrary.org/login?url=https://search.ebscohost.com/login.aspx?direct=true&db=psyh&AN=2012-11370-016&site=eds-live&scope=site

Braun, T., Rohr, M. K., Wagner, J., & Kunzmann, U. (2018). Perceived reciprocity and relationship satisfaction: Age and relationship category matter. *Psychology and Aging*, 33(5), 713–727. https://doi-org.ezp.waldenulibrary.org/10.1037/pag0000267

Business Dictionary, (2018). Retrieved from http://www.businessdictionary.com/definition/open-ended-question.html

Cambridge English Dictinary (2018). Definition of dominate. Retrieved from https://dictionary.cambridge.org/us/dictionary/english/dominate

Chapman, G. (2018). Who will take the lead. The Five Love Languages. Retrieved from https://www.5lovelanguages.com/2018/07/who-will-take-the-lead/

Cox, D. W., & O'Loughlin, J. (2017). Posttraumatic stress mediates traditional masculinity ideology and romantic relationship satisfaction in veteran men. *Psychology of Men & Masculinity*, 18(4), 382–389. https://doi-org.ezp.waldenulibrary.org/10.1037/men0000067

Dean M., B., Eric C., W., & Thomas B., H. (2011). The association of childhood trauma with perceptions of self and the partner in adult romantic relationships. *Personal Relationships*, (4), 547. https://doi-org.ezp.waldenulibrary.org/10.1111/j.1475-6811.2010.01316.x

Drollinger, T. (2018). Using active empathetic listening to build relationships with major-gift donors. *Journal of Nonprofit & Public Sector Marketing*, 30(1), 37–51. https://doi-org.ezp.waldenulibrary.org/10.1080/10495142.2017.1326336

Fahs, B., Swank, E., & McClelland, S. I. (2018). Sexuality, pleasure, power, and danger: Points of tension, contradiction, and conflict. *In APA handbook of the psychology of women:* History, theory, and battlegrounds., Vol. 1. (pp. 229–247). Washington, DC: American Psychological Association. https://doi-org.ezp.waldenulibrary.org/10.1037/0000059-012

Franklin, C.W. II (1984) . Black male-black female conflict individually caused and culturally nurtured. *Journal of Black Studies*. 15 (2) 139-154.

Holden, V.M., (2018, July 25). Slavery and America's legacy of family separation. Retrieved from https://www.aaihs.org/slavery-and-americas-legacy-of-family-separation/

Holland, K. J., Lee, J. W., Marshak, H. H., & Martin, L. R. (2016). Spiritual intimacy, marital intimacy, and physical/psychological well-being: Spiritual meaning as a mediator. *Psychology of Religion and Spirituality*, 8(3), 218–227. https://doi-org.ezp.waldenulibrary.org/10.1037/rel0000062

Hudson, N., Culley, L., Law, C., Mitchell, H., Denny, E., & Raine, F. N. (2016). "We needed to change the mission statement of the marriage": biographical disruptions, appraisals and revisions among couples living with endometriosis. *Sociology of Health & Illness*, 38(5), 721–735. https://doi-org.ezp.waldenulibrary.org/10.1111/1467-9566.12392

Jit, R., Sharma, C. S., & Kawatra, M. (2017). Healing a Broken Spirit: Role of Servant Leadership. Vikalpa*: The Journal for Decision Makers, 42(2)*, 80–94. *https://doi-org.ezp.waldenulibrary.org/10.1177/0256090917703754*

Karbelnig, A. M. (2018). The geometry of intimacy: Love triangles and couples therapy. *Psychoanalytic Psychology*, 35(1), 70–82. https://doi-org.ezp.waldenulibrary.org/10.1037/pap0000144

Kennedy, S. C., & Gordon, K. (2017). Effects of integrated play therapy on relationship satisfaction and intimacy within couples counseling: A clinical case study. *The Family Journal*, 25(4), 313–321. https://doi-org.ezp.waldenulibrary.org/10.1177/1066480717732169

Knobloch, L. K., & Delaney, A. L. (2012). Themes of Relational Uncertainty and Interference From Partners in Depression. *Health Communication*, 27(8), 750–765. https://doi-org.ezp.waldenulibrary.org/10.1080/10410236.2011.639293

Lammers, J., & Maner, J. (2016). Power and attraction to the counternormative aspects of infidelity. *Journal of Sex Research*, 53(1), 54–63. https://doi-org.ezp.waldenulibrary.org/10.1080/00224499.2014.989483

Marshall, E. M., & Kuijer, R. G. (2017). Weathering the storm? The impact of trauma on romantic relationships. *Current Opinion in Psychology*, 13, 54–59. https://doiorg.ezp.waldenulibrary.org/10.1016/j.copsyc.2016.04.013

McClelland, S. I. (2017). Vulnerable listening: Possibilities and challenges of doing qualitative research. *Qualitative Psychology*, 4(3), 338–352. https://doi-org.ezp.waldenulibrary.org/10.1037/qup0000068

McGraw, P. (2018). Post-traumatic stress disorder: The symptoms. Retrieved from https://www.drphil.com/advice/post-traumatic-stress-disorder-the-symptoms/

Merriam-Webster. (2018). Power definition. Retrieved from

https://www.merriam-webster.com/dictionary/power

Milan D Bjekic, Sandra B Sipetic-Grujicic, Hristina D Vlajinac, & Aleksandra M Nikolic. (2018). Oral sex related knowledge and oral sex behavior among homosexual and heterosexual men in Belgrade: A cross-sectional study. *Indian Journal of Dermatology, Venereology and Leprology*, Vol 84, Iss 5, Pp 563-568 (2018), (5), 563. https://doi-org.ezp.waldenulibrary.org/10.4103/ijdvl.IJDVLpass:454_17

Owen, J., Quirk, K., & Manthos, M. (2012). I Get No Respect: The Relationship Between Betrayal Trauma and Romantic Relationship Functioning. JOURNAL OF TRAUMA & DISSOCIATION, 13(2), 175–189. https://doi-org.ezp.waldenulibrary.org/10.1080/15299732.2012.642760

Psychology Today Retrieved from https://www.psychologytoday.com/us/basics/emotional-intelligence

Ricks, S. A. (2018). Normalized Chaos: Black Feminism, Womanism, and the (Re)definition of Trauma and Healing. *Meridians: feminism, race, transnationalism,* 16(2), 343+. Retrieved from http://link.galegroup.com.ezp.waldenulibrary.org/apps/doc/A542968074/EAIM?u=minn4020&sid=EAIM&xid=839741b5

Schwartz, A. (2014). The neurobiology of transgenerational trauma. Retrieved from https://drarielleschwartz.com/the-neurobiology-of-transgenerational-trauma-dr-arielle-schwartz/

Smith, J. P. (2018). Trauma in relationships. Red Table Talk. Retrieved from https://www.facebook.com/redtabletalk/videos/domestic-abuse-when-love-turns-violent/1677913888981847/

Taylor, D.C., McClain, M.R. (1997). Conflict in Black male/female relationships. CSUSB ScholarWorks. Retrieved from https://scholarworks.lib.csusb.edu/cgi/viewcontent.cgi?referer=https://www.google.com/&httpsredir=1&article=2322&context=etd-project

Wade, R. (2018). The difference between not talking and truly listening. *The Feminine Woman*. Retrieved from https://www.thefemininewoman.com/the-difference-between-listening-and-not-talking/

Wade, R. (2018). Why do men really love blow jobs. *The Feminine Woman*. Retrieved from https://www.thefemininewoman.com/why-men-love-blow-jobs/

Watson, K. W. (2017). Effective Listening: Five Lessons from the Best. Journal of Christian Nursing, 34(3), 159. Retrieved from https://ezp.waldenulibrary.org/login?url=https://search.ebscohost.com/login.aspx?direct=true&db=edo&AN=124269152&site=eds-live&scope=site

Woolf-King, S. E., & Maisto, S. A. (2015). The effects of alcohol, relationship power, and partner type on perceived difficulty implementing condom use among African American adults: an experimental study. *Archives of Sexual Behavior*,44(3),571–581. https://doi-org.ezp.waldenulibrary.org/10.1007/s10508-014-0362-7

Wright, B.L. (2018). What are some non-sexual forms of intimacy? Retrieved from https://www.sharecare.com/health/sex-and-relationships/non-sexual-forms-of-intimacy

ABOUT THE AUTHOR

Troya Bishop is regarded as a fierce fighter and advocate for social causes. With over 21 years of experience in advocacy and non-violent protests, she has extensive experience in long-term strategic planning, with various civil and human rights campaigns.

She has been active in the social justice movement since attending NAACP meetings in Tuscaloosa, Alabama as a child. In middle school she was nicknamed, "Ole' Badd Troya", by classmates, because of her unique ability to get adults to listen, and because of her feisty, but sweet spirit. As an adult, Troya served as a Leadership Commissioner (2010-2012) and Crisis Committee Chairperson in Rev. Al Sharpton's Atlanta office of National Action Network (2009-2012). Under the leadership of Rev. Sharpton, Troya was a key liaison in many cases regarding human rights violations. She was essential in the mobilization efforts to stop Troy Davis' execution by coordinating press campaigns, rallies, protests, and collaborating with many other organizations.

As a believer in the nonviolent approach to crisis resolution, Troya identifies closely with the philosophies of Dr. King and Mahatma Ghandi. Non-violent activism was a key approach to social change that she learned while earning her B.S. in Communications from Howard University. While completing her Masters of Education at Tennessee State University, her research was heavily comprised of non-violent behavior modification strategies for working with children with behavior disorders. She is developing her skills to motivate and teach adults, as she earns her Doctorate of Education in Higher Education & Adult Learning from Walden University.

For more information about Ole' Badd Troya, or to connect with her, follow her on social media or visit her on IMDb

Theanswerstoracism.com

Facebook – Troya Bishop - @OleBaddTroya

Instagram - @OleBaddTroya

Twitter – TheAnswers2

Email – theanswerstoracism@gmail.com

www.ingramcontent.com/pod-product-compliance
Lightning Source LLC
Chambersburg PA
CBHW031222090426
42740CB00007B/663